People Jesus met

Story by Penny Frank

Illustrated by John Haysom

THE LION
STORY BIBLE

45

TRING · BELLEVILLE · SYDNEY

The Bible tells us how God sent his Son Jesus to show us what God is like and to tell us how we can belong to God's kingdom.

The stories in this book are about some of the people Jesus met. In your Bible you can find them in the Gospels.

Copyright © 1984 Lion Publishing

Published by
Lion Publishing plc
Icknield Way, Tring, Herts, England
ISBN 0 85648 770 8
Lion Publishing Corporation
10885 Textile Road, Belleville,
Michigan 48111, USA
ISBN 0 85648 770 8
Albatross Books
PO Box 320, Sutherland, NSW 2232, Australia
ISBN 0 86760 555 3

First edition 1984

Printed and bound in Hong Kong
by Mandarin Offset International (HK) Ltd.

British Library Cataloguing in Publication Data

Frank, Penny
People Jesus met. – (The Lion Story Bible; 45)
1. Jesus Christ – Miracles – Juvenile literature   2. Bible stories, English – N.T.
I. Title   II. Haysom, John
226'.709505   BT366

ISBN 0-85648-770-8

Library of Congress Cataloging in Publication Data
1. Jesus Christ—Influence—Juvenile literature. 2. Jesus Christ—Friends and associates—Juvenile literature. 3. Jesus Christ—Miracles—Juvenile literature
[1. Bible stories—N.T.] I. Haysom, John, ill. II. Title. III. Series: Frank, Penny. Lion Story Bible; 45.
BT304.3.F73 1984   226'.09505
84-17090
ISBN 0-85648-770-8

The children in Galilee loved to be with Jesus.

'Let's go and find Jesus,' they said.

Their parents often left the work they were doing in their homes or fields and went with them to see Jesus.

Jesus was never too busy to talk to people.

The crowds enjoyed watching Jesus heal the sick people. Sometimes a man walked for the very first time, or a person who had been blind pointed at the trees and flowers he could suddenly see.

The people listened when Jesus
answered difficult questions and
explained about God's kingdom.

Do you remember the man called
Nicodemus? He was an important man
who had a lot of questions to ask Jesus.
He was worried in case other leaders
saw him going to Jesus.

So Nicodemus waited until night-
time.

'You must believe me, Nicodemus,' said
Jesus firmly. 'God loved the world so
much that he sent me, his own Son, to
give eternal life to everyone who
believes in me.'

Nicodemus went away with a lot to
think about.

He never forgot the day he met Jesus.

There was a man who had never
walked because his legs did not work
properly. So his four friends took him
to see Jesus.

They almost gave up when they saw
the crowds.

Then one of them had a good idea.

'Let's put him down through that hole in the roof,' he said.

Jesus healed the man, and he even helped his friends carry his own bed home. That man never forgot the day he met Jesus.

Do you remember the woman from Samaria who met Jesus at the well? She was surprised when he offered her a drink of water.

'You have no bucket to dip into the well,' she said.

'The water I can give you is God's water of eternal life. In God's kingdom no one need ever be thirsty again.'

The woman went back to the town.

'Jesus must be God's Son,' she told the people. 'He knew all about me.'

And she never forgot the day she met Jesus.

Some people were very shy about
asking Jesus for help.

One woman needed Jesus to heal her.
She had been ill for a long time. She
spent all her money to see the doctors
but none of them could make her better.

The woman watched Jesus healing the
sick people.

'Even if I could touch his coat I
would be well,' she thought.

So she reached out to touch the coat
of Jesus as he went by. She was better!
Jesus had healed her.

She never forgot the day she met
Jesus.

Jairus ran to fetch Jesus. His little girl was dying and no one could make her better.

But there were so many people around Jesus that by the time they arrived at the house, the little girl had died.

On t
skin
The
their
'Tha
    O
Jesu
    H

Everyone in the house was crying. Jesus went into the little girl's room and took her hand.

'Get up now,' he said. Everyone was amazed when she got up alive and well.

Jairus never forgot the day he met Jesus.

An important man came to Jesus.

'You keep telling us about the life of God's kingdom,' he said. 'I want to know more about it. How can I have this life?'

Everyone waited to hear what Jesus would say. They all wanted to know that answer.

'You love God and do as he says–but I think you love your money more than you love God,' said Jesus. 'If you gave it all away you would be ready to have God's life.'

The man went away very sad. He couldn't bear to give away his money because he was very rich.

That man never forgot the day he met Jesus.

Blind Bartimaeus sat by the side of the road to Jericho. Everyone knew him.

When he heard Jesus coming he shouted loudly, 'Jesus, listen to me.'

The people all said, 'Be quiet,' but he shouted all the more loudly.

Jesus stopped.

'What do you want me to do?' he asked.

'If only I could see,' said the blind man.

'You shall,' said Jesus, 'because you believed in me.'

Suddenly Bartimaeus could see how beautiful the world was.

He never forgot the day he met Jesus.

22

Everyone who met Jesus went away to tell other people about him.

None of them ever forgot the day they met Jesus.

The Lion Story Bible is made up of 52 individual
stories for young readers, building up an understanding
of the Bible as one story–God's story–a story for all
time and all people.

The New Testament section (numbers 31-52) covers the
life and teaching of God's Son, Jesus. The stories are
about the people he met, what he did and what he
said. Almost all we know about the life of Jesus is
recorded in the four Gospels–Matthew, Mark, Luke and
John. The word gospel means 'good news'.
     The last four stories in this section are about the
first Christians, who started to tell others the 'good
news', as Jesus had commanded them–a story which
continues today all over the world.

In *People Jesus met,* the story of Nicodemus comes
from John's Gospel chapter 3; the four friends from
Mark, chapter 2; the woman at the well from John,
chapter 4; the sick woman and Jairus' daughter from
Luke, chapter 8; the ten 'lepers' from Luke, chapter 17;
the rich young man from Matthew, chapter 19; blind
Bartimaeus from Mark, chapter 10. These are just a few
of the many Gospel stories of people whose lives were
changed because they met Jesus. Jesus still changes
lives today: no one ever forgets the day they first meet
Jesus.
     The next story in the series, number 46: *Jesus the
King,* tells how Jesus rode in triumph into Jerusalem,
just a few days before he was put to death.